W. WALL

A SUMMARY OF HISTORICAL SKETCHES ON THE FORMATION OF THE RUSSIAN LAWS

Elibron Classics
www.elibron.com

Elibron Classics series.

ISBN 1-4021-9912-0 (paperback)
ISBN 1-4021-2396-5 (hardcover)

This Elibron Classics book contains the complete text of the edition published in 1841,
St. Petersburg.

FIRST PART

SUMMARY OF HISTORICAL SKETCHES from 1700 TO 1826

I ORIGIN OF THE INCORPORATION OF THE LAWS

The first idea of digesting the laws of the Russian Empire, and forming them into one single body belongs to Peter the Great.

By an ukase of February 18th 1700, it was ordered, to compare the code of 1649, with the acts of the legislature published since that period; viz: with the *novels* or new constitutions, (новоуказныя статьи) the ukases, and the decrees of the Council of Boyards.

A rapid glance over the constituent parts of the legislation of this period, will suffice to explain the intention and the motives of this undertaking.[1]

The general code of 1649 had recently given a permanent form of legislation, by incorporating all that it was deemed necessary to preserve of preceding laws. The main object of this code was, rather to present an orderly arrangement of those laws which already existed, than to remodel them, or devise new ones; but as from the hurried manner[2], and consequently contracted form in which the twenty five chapters composing the code had been framed, it was not possible to give to each branch of the laws the full and entire development of which it was susceptible, it was therefore understood, that whatever omissions or deficiences might exist, they should be filled up and supplied at a future period. Hence, supplementary acts, under the various forms of

---

[1] The general history of the progress of legislation in Russia, from authentic sources, will be treated of in a special work, intrusted to the 2nd Section of His Imperial Majesty's Chancery.

[2] The code was commenced July 16th 1649, and terminated October 3rd of the same year. (The year then began in September) It was therefore completed in two months and seventeen days. (See the beginning of the code in the ukase which is annexed to it for publication.)

novels, ordinances and decrees of the council, appeared shortly after. The purport of each and all of these acts was, to aid in developing the code, but in deviating from this object, they soon diverged into an opposite direction. Being not oftentimes in direct opposition one to the other, they, for the most part displayed a striking contradiction with the spirit of the laws. Still their numbers continued increasing, and in the course of half a century, they amounted to several volumes. Jurisprudence, so heterogeneous, so incoherent and contradictory, could not fail of creating doubt and confusion in the application of the laws. Such was the state of the legislation, at the period when it attracted the attention of Peter the Great. It was deemed necessary to arrest the progress of such disorder, and the remedy which he employed, was the only effectual one. But the task which he had conceived to be a determinate work, which might be accomplished in a short space of time, became in the end, a kind of permanent institution, which under the form of commissions successively formed and re-organized lasted, almost without interruption, till 1826, a period of 126 years.

II
THE FORMATION AND ORGANIZATION OF THE COMMISSIONS

First Commission of the year 1700.

This commission was composed of different members of the Supreme Council, and of secretaries specially appointed to the office. In taking as a basis the code of 1649, its object was to collect and form into one single body all the laws then in force. The time of its duration is uncertain. The result of its labours in 1703, consisted in a project of concordance, unfinished, on three chapters of the code.

Second Commission of the year 1714.

Peter the Great seeing the little progress the commission made, thought it advisable to abolish by a general enactment or order, every subsequent act which did not agree with the code. But hence, naturally arose the question: Which are the acts which come under this category?

To resolve this question, the Senate was charged to examine them, and to add to the code such acts as might assist in completing it. During the years 1714 to 1718 inclusive, the chanceries to which the task. had been confided, composed ten chapters of what was called Code of Concordance, but they were not completed and remained without being revised or continued.

Third Commission of the year 1720.

The Code of Concordance advanced but slowly, and seemed not to give much promise of ultimate success. Hence in 1720, arose the idea of quitting the track. hitherto pursued, and of taking another course. The proposal was to digest a new code, by reforming-the old one, after the model of the Swedish code, and afterwards at a later period, of the Danish. It is easy to imagine what were the obstacles to these new measures, arising; from the dissimilarity of the languages, the want of experienced lawyers, the radical difference of the two systems of laws, and most of all, from the anomalies and contradictions in our legislation, which, not being as yet reduced into one entire body, presented no possible means of distinguishing with any certainty, between what was to be considered as a law in force, and what as abolished. Consequently on the death of the Empress catherine I., the new commission, after many useless efforts, was dissolved.

Fourth Commission of the year 1728.

In the succeeding reign, the original project of forming a Code of Concordance, was again revived; and although even the idea of its receiving still further modification, in order to improve the system of the laws generally, was not wholly renounced, yet the commission hoped to effect this, by means of its own experience, and without having recourse to foreign assistance. To this purpose, each government was called upon to send five deputies, men of probity and learning, to be chosen by the nobles. This is the origin of that arrangement, which upon a larger scale, took place in 1767.

The death of Peter the Second terminated the existence of this commission, before it had been enabled to commence its labours.

Fifth Commission of the year 1730.

This commission was founded upon the same basis as the preceding, but differing in the following respects, 1st, the number of its members was augmented, it had been even resolved to convoke deputies also, but this arrangement was afterwards changed; Sly, the plan of amending the laws by having recourse to foreign aid, entirely objected to by the preceding commission, was here revived; Sly and lastly, in the first, second and fourth commissions, the principal object consisted in effecting the agreement of the code with the antecedent acts, and in the amendment of the system of the laws being admitted only as a consequent; while here, on the contrary, the first consideration was the formation of a new code.

This code was commenced with the two chapters which at that time, were considered the two important; the one, on the Administration of Justice, the other, on Patrimonial Property. The composition of these two chapters, advanced very slowly. Yet the extreme confusion, into which the tribunals and various branches of the administration were thrown, by the disorder and uncertainty which existed in the legislation, made it absolutely necessary, in the first instance, without even waiting for the new code, to put the existing laws into order. Hence again arose in all its force the idea of a Code of Concordance, and in 1755, the Empress Anne, supposing that the measures previously employed towards its formation had brought it to a sufficient degree of completion, gave positive orders to have it promulgated.

But on preceding to execute this command, it was discovered that the work was very far from being completed; that several of its chapters composed during the two first commissions, had been already altered by the new ukases; that although extracts of the laws had been subsequently made, these extracts had no mutual connexion, and could not serve as a rule in giving decisions; that there were no other means of obtaining a true Code of Concordance, than by charging the tribunals and colleges themselves, to collect all the laws in force in their respective departments, and to form them under distinct heads, into separate bodies, which might afterwards be united into one. It is evident by this that the question was not decided, but only more divided. All the tribunals and colleges were over burdened with the weight of impending causes; and the chanceries clear, intelligible to all, and adapted to the present *time,* should be forthwith compiled.

Consequently, this same year a commission was appointed for the formation of a code. It was divided into one general commission, and several special commissions.

The general commission had for its object, the digest of a code, 1st, on the subject of Judicial Procedure, 2ly, on Criminal Matters, 3ly, on

Patrimonial Property, and 4ly, on Personal Rights.[3]

Special commissions were attached to the colleges, and were instructed to draw up certain regulations relative to administrative matters, so that there might be for every subject, a complete regulation divided into proper heads.

The revisal of the suggestions, both of the general commission, and the special commissions, was intrusted to the Senate.

The general commission terminated three parts of the work confided to it, namely, 1st, on Civil Procedure, 2ly, on Criminal Law, 3ly, on Personal Rights. The two first parts, in 1755, were brought before a general assembly of the Senate and Synod, and there examined; after which, they were presented accompanied with a report, in order to receive the Imperial sanction.[4]

---

[3] Under the term of Judicial Proceedings was then understood, not only a prescript of civil procedure, but also of all the statutes relating to bonds, contracts, offences and damages; and under the term of Patrimonial Properly or Patrimonial Chapter, was generally understood, statutes relative to the law of property, whether moveable or immoveable. Thus, in a word, the commission had to digest a civil code, and a penal code, with their respective procedures, as also the laws relative to Personal Rights.

[4] Such articles as bore any reference to canon law,

But this sanction was never granted.[5] The compiling of the law on Personal Rights lasted till 1760.

During all this time nothing had been dune by the special commissions, notwithstanding repeated intimations to that effect.

In the general commission itself, from the year 1756, the activity displayed during the two first years began insensibly to decline, till at length it nearly ceased altogether; and in 1760, the commission had no more than a nominal existence.

---

were signed, by the members of the Holy Synod. In the report of 1755, it was proposed among other things, that the new code should only come into force fire months after the day of confirmation, in order that the functionaries and assistants in the several tribunals and colleges, and Indeed all others, might not be exposed to the liability of committing any errors in consequence of the measure newly Introduced.

[5] Probably on the one hand, because it was intended to submit the subject in question, to the examination of the deputies, as appear* from what was done in the succeeding commission; and on the other, because among the proposed measures of the Penal Code, the punishment of death was admitted a penalty which, the Empress, without definitively abolishing it, had suspended from 1753 till 1754.

Seventh Commission of the year 1760.

Towards the close of Her reign, the Empress Elizabeth again directed her attention to the laws. The idea of the code once more presented itself, and hence resulted a new organization of the preceding commission. Two senators were appointed to superintend this operation. New members were named. All the special commissions were united to the general commission. It was resolved to terminate the laws relative to the Rights of Persons, to join them to the two first titles of the code, which had been prepared in the former commission, but which had never received confirmation; and then, to submit the whole to a new examination; and, that this revisal might be as complete and as exact as possible, it was thought necessary that the commission, as had been previously done, should have the services of deputies chosen from the nobility, clergy, and merchants.

During the earlier months of 1762, the deputies arrived from almost all parts. The sittings had opened; but they were soon interrupted by the journey to Moscow, on occasion of the Empress Catherine the Second's coronation, in the beginning of 1763. The deputies were dismissed, till such time as the code should be terminated.

Thus this commission did not complete the work it had commenced; and although its duration was prolonged till 1767, all its operations subsequent to the year 1763, were confined to correspondence, intimations and fruitless explanations. The special commissions also remained perfectly inactive.

Eighth Commission of the year 1767.

This commission carries with it the impress of grandeur it had received, not only from the extent of its organization, but particularly from the principles upon which it was founded. In the celebrated work of the Empress Catherine II., under the title of Instructions for the Compilation of the Code, these principles have been expounded.

The motives of its establishment, such as were published in the manifest, were as follows: 1st, the want of laws in many cases, and their superabundance in others, Sly, the commixture of permanent laws with laws temporary; 3ly, the obscurity and incertitude that lapse of time and frequent changes, as well as arbitrary interpretations had diffused into the spirit in which the ancient laws had been conceived; and 4ly, the difference between the times and manners of the past and the present.

The task assigned the commission was to compose a new code, in the most extensive signification of the word. To this effect, all the laws were classed into fifteen categories, embracing every branch of the legislation, except only what related to the army and navy.

The commission was composed as follows; it was divided into a general or grand commission and special commissions. Deputies from all the tribunals and all the administrations, from the nobility, from cities and towns, and even from bodies not belonging to the Greek, church, in all 565 persons, formed the general assembly. The special commissions were selected from among these same deputies, chosen by themselves to the number of five, for each commission: the latter had also a seat in the general assembly.

The special commissions amounted in all to nineteen. Of these, fifteen, according to the number of the compartments into which the laws had been divided, were occupied with the arrangement and digestion of the subjects. The four remaining commissions were distributed thus: one termed the Directing Commission over which the Attorney-General presided, was appointed to preserve general order, but more particularly to revise the individual productions, before they were submitted to the general assembly; another, the Commission of Expedition, was to correct the style of all the different compositions; a third, the Commission of Mandates, (instructions given by the constituents) whose duty was to discuss them and make extracts; and the last, a Commission of Concordance, established previous to all the others, was to collect the old laws, and make extracts from them.

This commission opened at Moscow on 31st. July 1767. On 21st August, it presented to H. I. Majesty an address of thanks, in the name of all Russia and on 29th Dec., five months after its opening, the members of the general assembly were dismissed to their homes till further commands. The special commissions alone remained.

These commissions were to take as a basis of their operations, 1st, the legislative instructions of the Empress; 2ly, the mandates or instructions given to the deputies of the tribunals and corporations; 3ly, the concordance of the laws expressly prepared.

Upon these bases, the commissions in the course of the five last years composed:

1. What were termed plans; viz:, summaries of the projects, merely containing a table of contents, and their principal divisions.

2. A few commissions presented, in the form

of essay, parts of the projects composed after these plans. But they were never revised or confirmed.[6]

In 1774, after six years' existence, this institution was abolished. All who composed it were dismissed; there remained alone one Chancery of Information.

Ninth Commission of the year 1797.

Experience having demonstrated the small success attending every attempt to form a new code, recourse was once again had to the old idea of a Code of Concordance.

Towards the end of 1796, an order was given

---

[6] The Commission of Schools, presented a project in 114 articles on the schools in towns and villages.

The Commission of the Posts, presented its views on the Post Establishment.

The Commission of Justice, — 45 chapter» on the Penal Code.

The Commission of Public Order. — 341 articles on the Organization of the Police.

The Commission of Personal Rights,— a few chapters on Family Rights.

The Commission of Personal Rights -— submitted 51 articles on the Nobility, 15 chapters on the Middle Classes, and a project on the condition of the Cossacks.

to unite all the acts of the legislature, and compile them into three books of laws: viz:, the Penal, Civil, and Financial. The commission organized for this purpose, received another denomination, that of commission for the concordance, and not for the composition of the laws. It consisted of four members under the direction of the Attorney-General. It produced, seventeen chapters on Civil Procedure, nine chapters on Patrimonial

Property; and thirteen chapters on the Penal Laws. These operations being merely preparatory, and presenting nothing complete, they were not even revised.

Tenth Commission of the year 1804.

In the beginning of the reign of the Emperor Alexander the question of the code attracted particular attention. One of the members of the Council of the Empire was appointed to examine the state of the preceding works, and to draw up a fixed plan for their continuation. This task was afterwards delegated to the Minister of Justice. A new order of proceedings was issued, and in 1804, a new commission was created.

The object of this commission was to digest new codes on every branch of the legislation, even on provincial law, taking as a basis the existing laws, and at the same time, to endeavour to complete and perfect them according to general principles of jurisprudence.

It was composed, of a council formed of the Minister of Justice and his deputy, and of three sections under the orders of referendees.

In 1809, the varions objects of its labours underwent another division, and its composition was at the same time partially altered. In 1810, consequent on the new organization of the Council of the Empire, it was transformed into an institution dependant on the latter. Its council was dissolved, and a director, one under whose orders it had been placed, was immediately to submit its proceedings to the Council of the Empire.

In 1812, this arrangement was again altered. In place of the director was substituted a council of three members, the oldest being president, under the immediate authority of a superior: this lasted till 1826.

The operations of the commission did not comprehend the entire circle which had been drawn out. They were confined to the Civil, Penal and Commercial codes. In these three parts, during the interval between 1804 and 1826, some few titles were composed in the form of projects, namely, three titles of the Civil Code, and one title on the Procedure; one title of the Commercial Code, and three titles of the Penal Code.

The articles of the project of the Civil Code, were at different periods referred to the revision of the Council of the Empire; but this examination was suspended, the first time on account of the third part of the project not having yet been completed; the second time, in 1815, the council finding it impossible to proceed in the revision of the new code, without having the actual legislation defined by a complete and systematic body of laws; and the third time, during the years 1821 and 1822, a greater part of the articles having been sent back to be corrected and remodelled; although all that the commission presented was revised.[7]

Besides the incomplete projects mentioned above, the following were the works undertaken by the commission:

1. According to a requisition of the Council of the Empire in 1815, the formation of a new Code of Concordance was commenced; fifteen parts or books on the two first titles of the Civil Code were composed. These are partly extracts,

---

[7] There were in all, 1443 articles revised: 821 were sent back or rejected.

and partly reprinted ukases, which have no other relation one to the other, than the common title under which they stand. A species of commentary, under the name of Elements of the Law, was intended to be added to it. A few chapters of it, relating to the two first titles of the Civil Code were composed.

2. In 1812, the commission represented to Its principal, the necessity of completing the collection of the legislative acts deposited in the archives; and in 1820, it submitted to him a plan relative to the means of forming a complete table of these acts, but this proposition was never carried into effect.

3. As according to the original principle of its organization, the commission was not only to embrace the general legislation, but also the provincial laws, it was resolved to appoint, local committees in the governments of the Baltic and the West, with instructions to prepare materials for the commencement of the latter work. Some of the committees commenced the task, others demanded and waited for a general plan and instructions in detail; but as they neither obtained the one nor the other, the work. was discontinued.

III
GENERAL ABSTRACT OF THE PROCEEDINGS OF THE COMMISSIONS

The measures undertaken by all the commissions, had embraced three principal objects; viz: to make a collection of the laws; to digest and reduce them into one single body; and lastly, to compose new codes.

1. Collection of the Laws.

Every commission usually commenced operations by the collection of the laws; and as this labour was recommenced by each fresh commission, it is evident that nothing had ever been completed. The difficulties on this head, were innumerable. At first, there were few acts printed, the chanceries were badly organized, the archives in disorder; the ukases for the most part were in manuscript, and forwarded directly to the tribunals and colleges concerned in their execution. For a long time there was no general depository for keeping and preserving the laws. It was not till 1802 that decided steps were taken to establish a depository at the Senate. The two following instances will suffice to give a clear idea of the state in which this department then was.

1. In 1763, the Senate judging it necessary to publish a complete collection of the laws, addressed itself to the commission, supposing that this collection was lying in its archives, or in those of the former commissions. The commission of 1764, replied that, so far from having such a collection, it did not even possess a complete table of acts, that it had but a few extracts, and these but very contracted, and that although it might by means of these extracts, form a table of contents, yet it could not guarantee its correctness.[8]

2. In 1812, after a lapse of more than forty years, the commission explained to its superior the necessity of collecting the laws. In 1820, the same representation was made, and at the same time a plan was submitted, relative to the means of making a complete table at once, in order to proceed afterwards to the discovery of the acts. These solicitations were of no avail.

---

[8] The Senate, on this reply, adopted other measures to form a collection of the laws. The ukases which had been collected, comprehended only the period between 1762 and 1770,—a collection otherwise very incomplete.

2. Formation of the Body of the Laws.

All the commissions generally, and even those whose principal object was to compose a new code, applied themselves to the process of digesting the laws, for they were aware that their vocation was to complete and perfect the legislation, and not to reconstruct the whole anew. But, as the commissions had different objects proposed to them, there was a consequent diversity of opinion as to the nature of the task imposed upon them.

Some of them (the 1st, 2nd, 4th, and partly the 5th) hereby understood a Code of Concordance, that is to say, a collection of the laws, in which the code of 1649 should occupy the principal place, and was to be developed and completed by the laws afterwards enacted. Such then being the received notion of these commissions, there remained two objects for them to accomplish, the one simple and easy, consisted in inserting the new ukases among the articles of the code; the other, much more important, consisted in causing the different articles to coalesce, in moulding them as it were together, and forming them into one homogeneous whole, by divesting them of all that was incongruous and contradictory. The first of these objects was attained; bat no steps whatever were taken towards the accomplishment of the second.

Other commissions conceived that in forming a digest of the laws, their office was to make extracts, for the simple purpose of facilitating the composition of the code. These extracts might have laid some claim to merit and utility, if, in the first place, they had been drawn from an accurate and complete collection of the laws, and if, secondly, they had been arranged under different heads of articles, and in an order suitable to their insertion in the code. But, such was not considered by the commissions the right course, on the contrary, their extracts presented nothing more than a confused compilation of statutes on any given subject, for instance, under the title of Inheritance, the extracts were compiled solely with respect to order of time, without any deductive reasoning, without being formed into articles, without regard to contradictions, and without any distinction between laws abrogated and those still in force. Such being the state of these compilations it is evident their utility must have been very limited, for what reliance could be placed upon them either for exactness or order.

3. New Codes.

All that was effected in the composition of these codes since 1754, consisted of mere outlines or rough draughts of projects, rather than projects themselves.

The two first projects complete and entire, appeared in 1754; the one relating to the Administration of Civil Justice, the other to Criminal Affairs, both were revised, but left without confirmation.

Things remained in this state till 1767. The commission of that year presented six projects, the contents of which have been previously mentioned. One of them alone relative to the Rights of Persons attained a certain degree of perfection, and as it seems, served as a basis to the charta afterwards granted to the nobility and the towns. All the others were nothing more than a few meagre sketches, considered even at that time, as scarcely deserving of notice.

On the dissolution of this commission, the idea of a new code, became extinct, and as it appears was never again revived during the reign of the Empress Catherine II. It was judged more desirable to complete and perfect the different branches of the laws separately, and to postpone the idea of a new general code, till such time as these branches should be more fully developed.

But in 1804, this idea was once more revived. The result of the proceedings of the commission has been already mentioned. Similar to all its predecessors, it never accomplished the task assigned to it.

Such was the fate of these institutions during the course of a whole century. From a general view of their labours, the following conclusions may be deduced.

The idea of collecting the laws into one body, and distributing them according to their contents is so simple and clear, that this measure hail been considered by almost every nation indispensable, as one of the first necessities of the state, in proportion as the numbers of the laws augmented. On one hand, it was universally felt that the laws, being the offspring of necessity and circumstance, could not be made after any fixed and determinate system, but on the other, it was by all admitted, that a legislation of so complicated and discordant a nature, must finally be reduced to uniformity, in order to facilitate its execution. Thus, the two forms of legislation are every where to be seen; — the one primitive and partial, the other, posterior and systematic.

To have a uniform and regular body of laws

was invariably desired in the Empire of Russia, under every reign, whatever its diversity of aspect and duration, it never ceased to be felt. The form and means of realizing it were differently conceived; some advocated the collection of the laws; others a new codification; but the principal design, was ever the same; namely, a clear, methodical, and uniform system of laws.[9]

All who had been called upon to execute this task, for the most part, applied themselves to the undertaking with zeal. It. is not then to inactivity that we must refer the cause of the delays and want of success; but to the circumstances of the time being, as well as to the organization of the measures adopted.

It is to the circumstances of the time, that we must attribute the necessity under which the government lay, of employing men who for the

---

[9] Nothing has been spared, to obtain the accomplishment of this design. The pecuniary expenses of the commissions, without mentioning gratuities and rewards, form a considerable sum. Statements of the cost of commissions previous to 1754, are not to be found in the archives, but since that period till 1836, the expenditure incurred amounts to the sum of 5,678,593 roubles banco, calculated according to the varying rate of exchange.

most part were overburdened with other occupations. Hence it resulted, on the one hand, that they were unable to devote themselves with assiduity to the subject, and on the other, that according to their order of service, they were frequently changed, and had to quit the commission, after acquiring but a very slight idea of the task which they had to perform. Those who succeeded them had to recommence a new study; it not unfrequently happened, that nearly all the members found themselves dispersed in other administrations, leaving only one compiler with two or three copyists. Thus the work. was commenced by all the commissions, but terminated by none. These reiterated changes of men and measures, continued till the last commission in 1804.

It is also to circumstances of the time, that we must refer another serious obstacle. Experience in legal matters is of the highest importance in the practical application of the laws; and the want of it cannot be supplied by any speculative knowledge whatever. But when we have to condense and reduce laws to a system, we must know their origin, their different orders, their connexion and mutual relation; here both theory and practice are needed. But from the progress and period of our civilization, this combination was rarely witnessed in any commission preceding 1804. Hence arose that confusion in their plans, that perpetual vaccillation in their execution. Often were they arrested by the most ordinary questions of law, long before theoretically decided.

Such were the obstacles arising from the time being; others proceeded from the defective organization in the undertaking.

Almost all the commissions imagined their task. an urgent one, but easy to be accomplished. Hence it happened, that nearly all commenced at the end of the work, without having prepared either the beginning or the middle. The very first commission furnished an instance of this. In the first year of its appointment, it composed the manifest which was, to accompany the publication of the code, whilst at the same time, scarcely three chapters of the latter were compiled. All of the commissions observed three periods in! their mode of proceeding; viz: first to collect the laws; then to digest them; arid lastly, to complete and perfect, them. But on commencing with the collection, they thought it easy, as they expected to find all done by their predecessors; and when experience proved to them the contrary, instead of devoting, of concentrating their whole attention to one fundamental object, and of bringing it to a conclusion, they, in order to terminate their labours the sooner, hurriedly passed on to the second degree, that is to say, began making extracts from a collection scarcely commenced. What confidence could be placed in such detached extracts, where the laws in force were all mingled and confounded with those annulled, where contradictions and omissions were continually occurring? It is well known that among laws belonging to the same branch, there not only exists a mutual connexion, but that this connexion frequently extends to other branches, and that consequently, to attain a perfect knowledge of the nature of the laws under any particular title, their combined examination is often required. But how is an examination of extracts so incomplete and unconnected to be accomplished?

In the mean time the further the commissions were removed from the period of their being first instituted, the greater the numbers of the laws which they had to disentangle, and that consequently, not only did it become more difficult to classify and form them into one body, but even to make a complete collection of them. In the commission of 1804, there was, generally speaking, infinitely more order than in any which preceded it. We have seen above that in 1812, it again represented the necessity of collecting the acts; and that in 1820, it contemplated forming a table of the laws preparatory to their collection.

This manner of comprehending and conducting the work, naturally explains the reasonable hopes which the commission might entertain of ultimate success, even by passing over the thorny paths of the middle part, of sketching out new projects rather than investigating old laws, a work of great labour, but rarely appreciated even when attended with success. But, to be convinced how preferable a slow and fatiguing pace is to precipitation, we have but to compare the new projects reduced by the commissions (mostly printed) with the body of the laws now published. The first glance will convince us, that these sketches do not embrace one half of their legitimate contents, and that which had been already defined and sanctioned by the laws. So true is it, that in the order of measures taken to regulate and amend a legislation, a new or reformed code, should necessarily be preceded by a correct and systematic body of the laws.

SECOND PART

HISTORICAL SKETCHES
from 1826 to the present time

By an ukase of Jan, 51st 1826, His Majesty the Emperor was pleased to declare that all the proceedings relative to the code should be conducted under His own immediate direction, and that consequently, the preceding commission should be transferred to the Second Section of His own private chancery.

Upon this new arrangement, there immediately arose the following principal questions for solution.

1st. To define with precision the nature and principles of codification.

2ly. To form a plan for the general division of the laws.

3ly. To arrange the preparatory steps in accordance with this plan, and then,

4ly. To arrange what had been completed.

The resolutions resulting from these questions, served as a basis for drawing the plan of the order, which the 2nd Section was to observe in its operations. The four following divisions will explain the manner in which the plan was gradually put into execution.

I
PRINCIPLES OF CODIFICATION

From the historical sketch contained in the first part, we perceive that the antecedent commissions were constantly wavering between two projects, one, a Code of Concordance, the other, a new code. By the former, they always understood an assemblage of the existing laws, digested according to their order of contents, without any alteration in their tenor. By the latter, they likewise understood an entire body of the laws in force, but one modified and completed.

Of these two systems, it was His Imperial Majesty's pleasure to adopt the former.

Thus was the principal question decided, and the nature of the work defined. But as there might be different methods adopted in its execution, it was afterwards found necessary to determine with more precision, what course was to be pursued.

The principal heads of a work of this kind are the following:

1. *A compilation of the laws by extracts*; that is to say, to collect verbatim parts of different laws relating to the same subject, and to form them into one body.

The extracts are either partial or general. Examples of the former may be seen in the ordinary course of civil or criminal processes. In practice they are of two kinds, the preparatory, and the definitive. In the preparatory extracts, the chancery reports in precise terms, and chronological order, every article which it finds in the laws applicable to the subject, observing at the same time one principal rule, never to make any omissions. For these omissions it is responsible, but more cannot be demanded of it, than an accurate distinction, a rigid choice between laws in force, and those the execution of which had been modified or altered, not in the letter, but by the spirit of subsequent laws. This regards the tribunal. Its business is to determine and apply, in accordance with this chronological statement, those laws which exactly and directly relate to the same matter, and which, being neither modified nor abrogated either literally. or by the tenor of subsequent laws, are still in full force.

The proceedings of the previous commissions offer examples of the latter kind; namely, general exstracts made fur entire chapters of the sections or titles on any given subject. These extracts were drawn up after two separate plans, sometimes according to the strict text, and sometimes by reference to the ukases, but invariably without any other connexion than that of chronological order, and without any distinction as to their obligatory force. This distinction was left to be determined by the commission, whose province it was to decide as to what articles were to be considered in force, what reformed, or what obsolete, so that considered in themselves, the exstracts were merely preparatory, and bore no definitive character.

2ly. *Commentaries.* Their general object is to develop according to a determinate system, some particular branch of the laws, their principles and the relation of their effects.

Examples of this kind of composition are innumerable. Their origin may be traced up to the writings (Institutiones et Commentaria) of the Roman lawyers. The Institutes of Justinian are of this class, although they have as much the force of law as any other portion of the Justinian Code.

3ly. *Manuals.* There is a vast number of compositions of this kind, both ancient and modern. They consist of condensed views of the laws on some given subject. In certain points they resemble the commentaries, but differ from them in two others, first, in that the commentaries are intended fur the instruction of youth, while the manuals are written as a guide to functionaries, by giving them a general idea of the nature of all matters falling within their department. Secondly, the commentaries usually comprehend an entire division of the laws, and observe more or less rigorously some adopted system; whilst the manuals, without any reference to the principles of the science, are drawn up with a view of facilitating the execution.

4ly. *Repertories.* They are generally written in alphabetical order, and are of two kinds, diffusive and condensed.

The former explain, as regards any given subject, the history of the earlier legislation, and its changes; also the power and principal spirit of the laws in force, and contain more or less in detail, accounts of the more remarkable private cases, and the judgments pronounced on them.[10]

---

[10] Specimens of this kind of composition are to be found in many Lalin, German, and French works, and particularly in Merlin's well known Repertory, and Favard of Langlade's Repertory. Works of this kind are, by English lawyers, called a Digest or law-Dictionary; as, for Instance, Comyns's Digest; and

The abridged repertories present a view of the laws on any given subject, by pointing out the continuation and chronological order of the laws according to their contents, as well as the date of their enactment. A repertory of this kind (указатель) is to be found annexed to the complete collection of the Russian laws published in 1850.

5ly. *Code of Concordance* (сводное уложеніе). Under this term was designated, as before observed, the codification commenced in 1700, by order of Peter the Great.

It was called *Code,* on account of the code of 1649 having been taken for its basis; and *Concordance,* because in its compilation, it was here intended to digest and unite all the laws subsequently enacted.

This work differs essentially from the extracts mentioned above. The name of *Concordance* was sometimes given to the extracts, but never that of *Code,* for they had neither its form, nor its connexion, and could be serviceable only as a preparatory step.

6ly. *Body of the Laws of Justinian.* It is known that the Justinian Code consists of three principal parts: the Institutes (Institutiones), the

---

Tomlins's Law Dictionary.

Pandects (Digesta), and the Imperial Edicts (Codex). These three parts united into one, and augmented by novels, finally received the appellation of Body of Laws (corpus juris).[11]

It is also known that the first part of this work is a treatise of Gains, which has undergone several modifications, and that the second is nothing more than a compilation of different fragments or extracts, selected from the writings of other celebrated lawyers of antiquity, — writings which from their importance, had acquired the force of law, even before Justinian. As to the third part, it is known to be merely a literal collection of the ordinances, rescripts, and responses, of the different Emperors, commencing with Adrian. It is arranged and distributed according to the principal subjects of legislation, but without any direct connexion of one article with another; for in each title, the acts are placed in the order of time of their publication, and not in the order of their mutual bearings.[12]

---

[11] This denomination was first given to them by the commentators, and afterwards by Den-nit Goltofred, in his edition of 1604.

[12] The Code of Justinian may be considered under two points of view: 1st, as a body of ancient laws; and 2ly, as a code reformed according to certain changes

On comparing together the different forms which the codification might assume, there can be on hesitation as to the choice. It is evident, that our Code of Concordance, in its earlier productions, and the Code of Justinian in its effective execution, alone present any thing of a legislative work. All other forms, — the manuals, the extracts, the repertories, and the commentaries, are only the works of individuals.

The nature and form of the Code were thus defined, it was to be a *corpus juris*, a general system of the laws, and in that sense, it was to embrace every part of the legislation in its fullest extent.

The motives upon which it was resolved to undertake the formation of a body of laws, and not the composition of a new code, are evident. They arise from the following considerations:

"When the laws," says Lord Bacon, "accumulating one upon another, have increased so as to form several bulky volumes, or have reached such a state of confusion, that it is found

---

made in the ancient laws, partly by Justinian himself (quinquaginta de-cisiones), and partly by compilers under his authority. The first point of view is the principal one, as embodying the very essence of the collection.

absolutely necessary wholly to remodel them (de integro retractare), and to form them into a sound and well constituted body (in corpus sanum et habile redigere), let the latter be the first care of the legislator, one which must precede every other (id ante omnia agito), and let him bear in mind, that it is a work of the utmost importance, as well as of the utmost difficulty (atque opus ejus modi opus heroicum esto)."[13] This advice evidently intended for England, may with as much, and even more propriety, apply to our own country.

Almost all nations, on their having made some progress towards actual civilization, have alike succeeded to a rich inheritance, — the Roman Laws.[14] It is proved, tpat these laws never ceased to be in use in the west of Europe, but they acquired new force, and became nearly general, about the beginning of the sixteenth cen-

---

[13] De Augm. Soient. tractatus de Jost. univers. Aphor. 59.

[14] England received less of this inheritance than any other pople; there, what is called Justinian Law has no effect in some Courts of Justice, and even then with restrictions. (Blackstone's Comment. Introd. Section III.). The Stales of Scandinavia are also, In a great measure, governed by their own laws.

tury; and it must be here remarked, that this treasure has not descended to modern nations, in that confused state and formless mass, in which it was even at Rome, but in a regular and complete body of laws, first Theodosius's and afterwards Justinian's. Thus, even before each special necessity and circumstance arose, laws had been prepared to regulate and determine them; laws, moreover, devised by profound knowledge, tried by long experience, and sanctioned by ages. Nothing more remained than to study them, and to explore their deep and inexhaustible source. In those cases, where these laws might appear incompatible with the spirit of the nation, or with the circumstance of the time, there, customs and traditions were at hand to supply their place. Thus, in this part of Europe, there were two abundant sources of legislation, — the Roman Laws, and the customs and experience of each particular nation.

Russia was destined by Providence to another fate. Nothing of the Roman inheritance has reached us. Our legislation has been wholly drawn from our own national sources, from our customs, traditions, and experience. The imitations which appeared at the beginning of the eighteenth century, cannot here be taken as any serious exception. They related to but one single branch of the laws, viz, to the organization of constituted authorities, and moreover, they were not borrowed directly from the Roman institutions, but from the German. Laws civil and criminal, laws of administration and internal police, — all were to be created and reconstructed, and from our own materials.[15]

It is from this very difference of legislative sources, that the peculiar difficulties, specially inherent in the order of our legislation and administration, originate.

These difficulties are not insurmountable.

---

[15] In the code of 1649, there is a small number of articles, which seem to bear some resemblance to the Canon law of the Greek Church (Pedalion). There are others too, which appear similar to the Lithuanian statutes. The former resemblance is easily explained, by the origin of Canon Law, and its introduction among us; and the latter, by the consideration that the Lithuanian statutes were originally written in Bass, and that they might have been, before the publication of the code, more or less in use in our provinces bordering on Lithuania. It is besides evident, that these points of resemblance do not form an exception to the general principle, and by no means authorise the conclusion, that there exists a direct relation between oar legislation and the Roman laws, or the Code of Justinian.

Application, habit, and experience, have hitherto conquered them. When the vital powers of a state are ever progressing and augmenting, when the agricultural, commercial, and manufacturing interests of this state are continually increasing in power and extent; what can be a more irrefragable proof that order and stability must prevail in the execution of its laws? Evidence, so general, so convincing, can never be shaken by any accidental exceptions whatever. But the more incontestable this is, the more does it prove, that laws would have acquired greater efficacy, that their application would have been more easy, that the choice of those intrusted with their execution would have been more judicious, had not their action been impeded by difficulties resulting from their complexity. Let us point out the principal of these difficulties.

1st. *Difficulties in giving decisions on Judiciary and Administrative Matters.* In all those states were the Roman Law prevailed, few cases occurred, especially in civil ones, which had not been foreseen and determined by the laws, their number being so great, and their extent so well defined. Here, then, judgment might be pronounced, and might be simply carried into effect, without having recourse to the legislature, here, might it be established as a principle, that where a law was not clear or precise, the judge should have authority to pass judgment, according to the dictates of sound sense, namely, from general principles of law, for these principles already existed in the body of the Roman Laws, and had been confirmed by time and experience.

With us, on the contrary, the number of the laws was at first insufficient, and the judge found himself continually obliged to refer to the legislature. Hence, that mass of detached ukases, and decrees of the Council of Boyards. Under such a state of legislation, it was not practicable to allow the judge to pass decisions according to general principles of law, for these principles were no where established. When afterwards the number of the laws augmented, other difficulties then arose, from their complexity, their incongruity, and uncertainty. These were difficulties, perhaps, even more serious than the want of the law itself; for it is here, particularly, that chicanery, false interpretations, and arbitrary decisions, veiled under the semblance of justice, are concentrated, hence the origin and moving cause of that perpetually increasing number of interpretations and decisions, which in their turn produced new complication. What are the means of preventing this interminable confusion? None other than to classify the laws, and form them into one entire and homogeneous body.

We here subjoin another remark. If the complication of the laws obstructs the progress of business in the interior of the empire, how much greater must this impediment evidently be in such provinces as enjoy particular laws of their own, where the general laws must incessantly be made to correspond with the local statutes, which are themselves both unconnected and discordant. The only means of obviating these difficulties is, to reduce both the one and the other into regular bodies; for it is by this alone that their distinguishing features may be seized, and their apparent contradictions removed.[16]

---

[16] Our actual legislation consists of 35,000 acts; nearly one half of which, being either abrogated, or modified, by subsequent acts , or containing only repetitions, are mere matters of history. This superabundance, by the fatiguing research it occasions, retards and encumbers the actual process of a came; as ten ukases must be quoted and referred to» in-stead of one or two positive acts, which, at the same time, opens a vast field to fraud and chicane. The body of the laws, by purifying this commixture, and retrenching, all repetitions, places the judicial administrator In the right path ; if he caunot wholly eradicate fraud, he can at least powerfully limit and restrain it.

2ly. *Difficulties in the completion of the Laws.* In the existing order, there are two modes of completing them, namely, by official interpretations and supplements, as occasion demands, and by enacting certain regulations.

Official Interpretations and Supplements are indispensable in every species of legislation, for no system of laws whatever, can foresee and predetermine all possible cases.[17] They form, as it were, its vital and periodical movement, but this movement acts in two ways.

Where the laws have been collected into a body, the supplements and interpretations are then formed with more certainty and precision, every means being afforded to examine and' compare their relative bearings, and to become fully acquainted with their effects. They, by no

[17] This applies not merely to administrative regulations, but also to civil and criminal codes. Thus, for instance, complete as the French codes appeared, the decrees of the Court of Cassation, serving to interpret and elucidate its various acts, formed in 1826 twenty six volumes. (See Bulletin de Cassation, and les Codes Annotйs de Sirey). Whether these numerous interpretations are embodied as legislative enactments, or merely form a standard of appeal, the effect is always the same, so long as they are invariable, and generally received and acted upon.

means, create complication, as they all belong to the same system, and to the same spirit of legislation. Where, on the contrary', no body of laws exists, it is extremely difficult in their partially amended state, to embrace and determine all their consequences, besides that, in reforming one law, we incur the danger of altering or weakening-some other) which is more or less connected with it.

In this case every elucidation and supplement forming a separate act, necessarily increases the number of the laws, and renders their execution more difficult; for in such a state of things, it is seldom that any reliance can be placed on any law which is known, there being no absolute certainty that it may not have been modified, and again, these modifications are to be sought, as it were, at random. The constitutive parts of one and the same law, are often scattered throughout centuries, so that one of its clauses, for instance, appears in the code of 1649, another, in a regulation of 1741, and a third, in a supplement of 1830.

The Regulations impart a fresh form to the legislation, in those parts to which they are applied. It is a rule, that all changes which have been introduced into the earlier laws, should be cited in each regulation. But this rule, neither is nor can be followed, in the existing state of our laws. To effect tins, it would be requisite to refer to the anterior laws, to determine with precision their mutual bearings, to mark with accuracy whatever had been modified or explained; — a very laborious operation, and in the rapid course of administration, almost impossible. Hence it happens, that instead of precise directions, every regulation terminates in the following formule: "whatever is contrary to this regulation, in the antecedent laws is annulled; and all that is conformable to it, remains in all its force". It would be superfluous to enumerate the perplexity, the uncertainty, the explanations, and epistolary correspondence to which this confusion gives rise, as a natural and necessary consequence.

In addition to the official interpretations and the regulations, there is a third mode of perfecting the laws, namely, by means of a new codification. We have already explained the result of all that was undertaken on this subject, during; the course of a whole century, as well as the causes which impeded its success, the chief of which was, the precipitate manner in which the latter part of the work was commenced, before that which immediately preceded it had been prepared. If, in a complicate and heterogeneous legislative system, it is found difficult to interpret and complete the laws by particular regulations, how can the digest of a new and entire code be attempted. In almost every country where new codes have been undertaken, the laws, for many centuries past, have been resting on the broad and solid base of the Justinian Code, and upon this same base, has a new edifice been constructed.

3ly. *Difficulties in the Study of the Law*, It is known that legal knowledge is of two kinds: the one, practical, the result of experience in the management of causes, the other, systematic, acquired only by tuition. The latter kind it is impossible to attain, unless the laws have been previously classified and collected into one regular body.[18]

---

[18] England, apparently, presents an exception to this rule. There is no entire body of the English laws, but there are digests of the statutes. No code has ever been published by the government, although the want of one was long since experienced, not only by Bacon, Hales, and Hobart, but by the Parliament itself in 1660, and 1666; and more lately, (in 1796, 1803, and 1820) the necessity of a code was often felt and acknowledged, in several committees both of the Upper and Lower Houses. (See the Digest of the Statutes by Tyrwhitt and Tyndal, Preface, 1822.) There is, however, a vast number of compilations and

commentaries by private indi viduals, which, from time and use, have acquired an authority equal to that of a book. of the laws. Such are the works of Comins, Burn, Coke, Hales, Hawkins, Russell, and particularly the Commentaries of Blackstone. There exist, besides, very extensive private collections, containing the reports of adjudged cases, which reports, (in England termed Precedents) have the force of law, and constitute the principal part of what is called Common law. It is from these sources, without altogether neglecting those of the Boman Law, and from practical experience in legal process, that a knowledge of English law is derived. How far a study of this nature may be advantageous or inadequate, how far it might be desirable to have it superseded by a compilation of all the detached part» of the legislation, is a question warmly debated in England itself, and still remains undecided. This forms part of the grand question on Codes, lately discussed by lawyers, particularly In England and Germany. The principal feature» of the argument, on both side», may be found in Bentham's works, and especially In Dumont's Analysis of the latter, De L'Organizatlon Judiciare et de la Codification; in Sevigni's celebrated work, Beruf unserer Zeit fьr Gesetzgeburg; in Cooper's Letters sur la Cour de la Chancellerie d'Angleterre; and in Meyer's work sur la Codification. The limits of this sketch, do not allow of a minute examination of the question, which indeed does not properly belong to the present subject. The whole weight of the argument

Throughout all Europe, what is called the Roman Law is taught; but nearly in all parts of Europe, the Roman Law is, or was, for a long time in force. The existing laws are consequently studied; and for the greater part, from the very code in which they are contained. Where new codes have been introduced, these codes are studied,[19] without altogether neglecting the Roman Laws, as being the sources from which they were drawn.

With us, the zeal of our lawyers has often induced them to attempt to systematize that which is called Russian Law; — efforts worthy of all praise and encouragement, but of small value as to the advancement of the study itself. How indeed, is it possible to form a systematic body of didactic jurisprudence, without an accurate

---

bears upon the new codes, which, as it were, abrogate all that previously existed, and similar to the Justinian Code, close up every other source of legislation. It refers not to a body of the laws, such as we have at present, which, while it gives the literal sense of the law, without any change whatever, at the same time elucidates-rather than obscures its origin, and being accompanied with a complete collection of the very text of the laws, renders their intent evident, and intel, ligible to all.

[19] At Vienna, Paris, and Berlin.

knowledge of the laws collectively. To supply this defect, it was proposed to introduce the study of the Roman Law in our higher schools.

But the Roman Laws will always be foreign to us, and although by their number, and superiority in some respects, they might occupy an important position in the study of the law, yet a knowledge of them must be among us, considered as auxiliary, and not principal. Their system cannot serve as a basis to our own, for it is not in their system that their excellence lies; we know on the contrary how very defective it is in general, but they are distinguished by the accuracy of their practical spirit, — the remains of the profound knowledge and experience of antiquity.

It is not therefore from the Roman Law, nor yet from the isolated efforts of our lawyers, that *we* can expect to construct a solid foundation for a systematic study of the laws. It must be based upon a body of the laws, and will date its commencement from their publication. Until this is done, it would be useless to devise commentaries and prescriptions calculated to develop the science of national legislation.

Such are the principal causes, which determined the formation of a body of the laws, as being a work. necessary for the present, as well as a basis for gradual amelioration for the future.

After having defined the nature of the undertaking, what remained was, to decide upon the rules to be observed in the prosecution of it.

These rules are partly designated in the model selected for this purpose; namely, the Justinian Code. But principles more explicit and more general, have been drawn out by Bacon, and these same principles it was resolved to follow, admitting only some few necessary modifications. The principles laid down by Bacon, are as follows:

1st. "To exlude from a body of the laws, all those which might have become obsolete.[20] This principle was adopted with the limitation, that no law must be considered as abolished, until it be directly or indirectly abrogated by subsequent acts."

2ly. "To exclude every repetition, and instead of several statutes expressing one and the same law, only the most complete of them should be admitted."[21]

3ly. "To preserve the letter of the law, by extracting articles from the text itself, however small the fragments (per centones), and then to connect and digest them, for in a law, elegance

[20] Aphor 60.
[21] Ibid.

of style is of far less importance than strength and authority, and the warrant of authority, is antiquity. Without this, the body. of laws would be merely an academical composition, and not a body of positive laws."[22]

It was resolved to adopt this principle in the following sense: 1st, to express in the very words of the text, without the least alteration, those articles which were founded upon any one single act.[23] 2ly. To express the articles composed from two or three acts, in the terms of the principal one, adding from the others such terms as might serve to complete or explain them. 3ly. To express in the articles drawn from several different acts, the collective sense and meaning, and 4ly, note with precision, under each article, the acts from which it was composed.

4ly. "The law which are too diffuse and di-

---

[22] Aphor: 62.

[23] The number of these articles is very considerable, a» for instance, in the book. on the organization of administrations, in the book. on taxation in kind, in various regulations of financial administration, Й1 the civil laws, testamentary titles, money contracts, inventories, and sales of properly, and in the greater part of the regulations respecting credit and commerce.

lated, must be abridged."[24] It was resolved to adhere to this principle in the following sense: ukases are for the greater part composed of three parts, namely, a statement of the subject-matter or case, which gives rise to the law, 2ly, the motives and grounds, and 3ly, the text itself of the law and its application. Of these three parts, it was determined to exclude from the body of the laws the two first, but to preserve the third according to the strict letter of the text, even when it might be sometimes possible to express it in a more concise manner, but this conciseness, would have been contrary to the preceding principle.

5ly. Of those laws which contradict each other, to select and adopt the best.[25]

The compilers of the body of laws might have exceeded their limits, had they taken upon themselves to decide which was the better of two contradictory laws. When two laws are contradictory, it is a rule with us, to follow and apply the more recent one, without any inquiry whether it be the better or not, for the earlier law is con-

---

[24] It is well known that no laws are more verbose than the English, and it is to this pro' litity that Bacon refers.

[25] Aphor. 60.

sidered abrogated, by the circumstance of its place being supplied by another. If the contradiction occurs in one and the same act, and has not been removed by any subsequent acts, in such a case, the legislative power alone can rectify the error. In a body of laws, one must rest satisfied, that each law presents itself in such form, as it exists in the original text, without any alteration or modification.

6ly. "The body of laws being thus formed, it is to be revised and examined by a competent authority, in order to be assured that new laws, under the appearance of early ones, have not crept in."[26] Conformably to this principle, it was resolved to submit each part of the undertaking to the examination of such departments of administration, as the matter more properly concerned. It was consequently determined to appoint a private committee of revision, in each department, and for the civil and criminal laws, to form a special committee composed of senators and other functionaries, of which the Minister of Justice was to be president.

7ly. Bacon proposes the formation of two bodies of laws; one, from what in England is called Common Law, and the other, from the

---

[26] Aphor. 63.

Statute Law.[27] This distinction does not exist with *us*, but we have laws which operate generally throughout the whole empire, and local laws, the action of which extends only to a few provinces. For this reason, it was resolve to unite all the laws of the former kind in the general code, and after classifying those of the latter, to form them into two separate; bodies of provincial laws: the one, for the governments of the' West, the other, for the governments of the Baltic.

8ly. Besides the above-mentioned principles, it was judged necessary to adopt the following: as a body of laws founding its legislative enactment on the past, cannot anticipate the future, and must therefore be liable to subsequent changes, since as new necessities arise, there must be new laws to regulate them, it is easy to foresee, that their continually increasing number would soon precipitate the legislation into the same state of confusion, from which it had been extricated. In order to obviate this serious inconvenience, it was resolved to render the compilation of the codes a permanent undertaking; to continue the body of the laws, and by means of a succession of annual exertions, to reduce the

---

[27] Aphor. 61.

different acts of the legislature, as they might be published, to one and the same system of regularity and uniformity. It is thus, that the edifice once constructed, may be heightened and enlarged, and at the same time preserve its cohesion, it" identity, and its principal proportions.

II
DIVISION OF THE LAWS

The body of the laws is divided, as follows, into eight codes.

The first code contains *Regulations relative to the Principles of forming Decisions on Administrative and Judiciary Cases.* These regulations are preceded by the fundamental laws of the empire, and, the statutes relating to the Imperial Family.

The second code contains the R*egulations respecting Homage or Taxation in Kind*; and comprises all matters relating to the raising of recruits, and certain labour taxes on the peasantry.

The third code comprises the *Regulations relative to the Administration of the Finances.* It embraces the regulations on taxation, and excise duties, the regulations on the customs, currency, mines, and salt works, regulations regarding forests, and letting of lands, etc. Here also will be inserted the regulations on responsibility and control, so soon as the proposed re-organization of this branch shall be completed.

The fourth code is composed of the laws relative to *Personal Rights.* It contains the rights of the nobility, clergy, citizens, wandering tribes, peasantry, and foreigners; as well as the regulations. concerning the acts of the civil power, and on the census.

The fifth code comprises *the Civil Laws:* 1st, the laws relative to family duties, marriage, paternal authority, guardianship, and trusteeship; the laws on real property, bonds, and contracts, and on civil procedure: 2ly, the laws on the boundaries of estates.

The sixth code contains *the Regulations on Political Economy*: such are the regulations concerning public credit, commerce, trades, and manufactures; on roads, buildings, assistance to be rendered in case of fire; and concerning the administrative economy in cities and towns, villages of the Crown, and colonies of foreigners. To this code also will be attached, the regulations on public instruction, so soon as this branch shall have been effectively remodelled.

The seventh code comprises the R*egulations*

of Internal Police: 1st, on the maintenance of public order, general superintendence, public health, quarantines; 2ly, the regulations on the prevention and suppression of crime, passports, vagabonds, prisoners, and exiles.

The eighth code contains the *Penal Laws*: 1st, on crimes, misdemeanours, and penalties, 2ly, on criminal procedure.

Such is the general division of the body of the laws. Our limits do not permit us to enter into a full statement of the contents of each code, they are, indeed, indicated by the heads under which they are placed.

The principles of this division, as explained in a few words, are the following:[28]

Two relative and connecting bonds or links are necessary in a state, in reference to political relations, and to civil relations.

---

[28] The question of a systematic division of the laws properly belongs to the theory, or what is «ailed, the philosophy of law, that is, to that part of jurisprudence which treats of the primitive ideas of the morality of actions, of duty, of equity, and of justice (жqui et justi) etc. An historical view of all that has been hitherto attempted towards the investigation of these principles, might occupy a conspicuous position in the general history of legislation. Here we can Merely point out their results and general features.

Political relations are either internal or external. At present we treat only of the former. The civil relations are those referring to family and property.

From the relations arise rights and obligations. Both one and the other are determined and confirmed by the laws.

Hence two orders of laws: viz:, political and civil.

I. Political Laws.

There are two classes of political laws, which, must not be confounded, they diner in their objects, and in the principles on which they are founded.

The laws *of the first class, determine* the nature of the political bond, and the laws which emanate from it.

It comprehends two kinds of laws, the *former* of which defines the origin and operative effects of sovereign power in the legislation and government, the *executive organs-,* or the institutions, and the *means-,* or resources of the state. The second kind defines the relative ties which bind subjects to the supreme power" according to their different conditions, that is, with respect to the share which is allotted them in the formation of the institutions, and the executive power of the state.

Hence spring four compartments or divisions of political laws.

1. *Fundamental Laws.*

2. *The Organic Laws.* These determine the composition of the institutions, their forms, and the limits of their authority.

3. *The Laws concerning the Powers of the State.* These are either personal or material. The personal are the military, governed by particular institutions of their own, or these forces are destined to provide for the different necessities of the state, under the form of taxation, which is regulated by general laws, under the name of *Regulations on Homage or Taxation in Kind.* The material powers consist in the revenue. The mode of its collection and employment, is determined by *Regulations on the Administration of Finance.*

4. *The Laws on Personal Rights.* They determine the rights and obligations of subjects, according to the degree of their participation in composing the institutions and forces of the state.

The political laws of the *second class guarantee* by measures of political order, the political and civil relations, and the rights which are derived from them. To this class belong:

1. The Preservative Laws, such as the Regulations of Police.

2. The Penal Laws.

II. Civil Laws.

The civil laws, as well as the political, are divided into two classes.

To the *first class* belong all the laws which *determine* civil rights, that is, the laws which regulate the order of family rights and obligations; 2ly, the laws which establish the order of the acquiring and possessing of property; and 3ly, the laws which determine the order of these latter rights in their particular relation to public credit, commerce, manufacture, etc.

Hence arise three compartments or divisions of civil laws.

1. *The Laws respecting Family Relations.*

2. *The General Laws on Property.*

These two compartments or divisions, are designated according to received custom, by the general name of civil laws. To these are subjoined the laws which regulate the system of marking the boundary lines of estates.

3. *The Special Laws on Property,* which, according to their principal object, are designated by the name of laws on public economy.

In the *second class* of these laws, are comprised those which *secure* the civil rights by measures purely civil. Such are:

1. *The Laws on Executive Measures in such Cases as do not admit of Litigation.*

2. *The Laws on Civil Procedure* in general, and particularly on that of the circumscription of estates and commerce.

3. *The Laws on the Civil Measures of the Executive.*

From the intimate connexion which exists between the civil laws, some belonging to the second class, are enrolled among those of the first.

Such are the principal bases of the division adopted in the body of the laws. By this it was hoped to attain a two-fold object, viz:, convenience in applying them in all practical matters, and a means of studying them systematically, so that the same books of laws, and not two different systems, might serve as a basis, both in the administration of legal business, as well as classical instruction.[29]

---

[29] The order of the contents of the body of the laws, is combined with the principles of their systematie division. The political laws in the first class are contained in codes I, II, III, *IV,* and each of their compartments occupies the place which is

III
PREPARATORY OPERATIONS

The preparatory operations consisted: 1st, of the collection of the laws, and 2ly, of a special review of each part, by means of historical concordances.

I. Collection of the Laws.

Peter the Great, in 1720, (April 29th) ordered the Senate to divide all the legislative acts lately promulgated, into provisional acts, and permanent acts. The former, he ordered to be entered into a separate volume, and the latter, after they had been classed according to the order of their

---

theoretically assigned to it. In adhering closely to this distribution, it would have been necessary to pass on to the second class of political laws; to the regulations of police, and to the penal laws, but as these laws constitute the general guarantee, both of the political relations as well as of the civil relations, it was necessary, first to present the laws which determined the civil relations, and consequently to proceed, after the first class of political laws, to the civil laws. (Codes V and VI). The entire body terminates with the political laws of the second class, the laws of police, and the penal laws. (Codes YII and VIII).

contents, to be appended to the organic regulations of the Colleges. This was the commencement of the collection of the laws. These acts were originally printed and published in one volume, without observing' the order of their contents, it comprised the ukases from 1714 to 1718; then, from 1719 to 1720; and lastly, the ukases of 1721. Here the collection ceased; and although afterwards resumed and continued till 1730, it was again interrupted, and remained untouched till 1760; it then advanced only as far as 1770.[30]

Such were the first attempts towards a complete collection of the laws. Considering them in their whole extent, they comprehended only 27 years of the 180, which had elapsed between the code of 1649, and that of 1831; these 27 years are not even completely embraced; for the collection begun under the reign of Peter the Great, and continued by a few publications up to 1750,

---

[30] At a more recent period, the late commissions undertook the publication of a collection of the laws, under the name of a Law Journal; but it lasted only from 1817 till 1820. In 1816, a distinct collection of laws and regulations relating to the military service alone, Was commenced at the former Staff Department of His Imperial Majesty.

contains merely the acts which relate to the regulations; but the regulations themselves concerning the army, and navy, the regulations of Colleges and other general acts, are not printed in it. The collection begun during the reign of the Empress Catherine II, between the years 1762 and 1770, was also, upon examination, found to be very incomplete.[31]

The necessity, however, of a complete collection, became every year more and more perceptible. Notwithstanding its omissions and deficiencies, the edition of the acts printed under the direction of the government, was frequently republished, their general circulation had however become exceedingly limited.

This circumstance induced different individuals to form collections on private speculation. They were at first in manuscript, and in this state were for many years circulated among legal men, and sold in sheets at a very high price. The first of these collections which was printed, appeared under the title of Dictionary of Jurisprudence, published in one volume in 1788, and reprinted in 1791. Soon after was published Tchoulkoff's celebrated Dictionary. To these

---

[31] Compare this collection with the acts of these same years in the complete collection of 1830.

succeeded several others, under the titles of Repertories, Annals, Systematic Collections, and various other denomination". The most remarkable of these compositions, is Maksimovitch's Repertory of the Laws; — the most remarkable both in regard to its superior extent, and to its having been the source from which most of the others were derived.

The principal fault of these collections is their incompleteness, and their textual and chronological inaccuracy.[32]

---

[32] *Their Incompleteness.* Without naming any oilier collections, in Maksimovitch's Repertory, the best and most extensive of them ally 48 whole years are wanting, from 1649 to 1803. Besides this, it was discovered, in the first place, upon examination, that many important acts had been omitted; thus, for instance, from the publication of the code up to June 5th 1714, the date of the abrogation of the new articles, (новоуказныя статьи), the Repertory contains only 1075 acts, and after a close examination of this period, it has been ascertained that it contains 2827. — Secondly, in several volumes, extracts or merely summaries under the titles of ukases, are found intermingled; nor is it unfrequent in the same Repertory to meet with extracts of the same acts, printed in different places and under different dates.

Their Incorrectness as to Date. Several acts are

To these two defects was added another. The publishers, instead of completing and continuing one of the principal collections, reprinted, for the most part, the same acts, transferring them from one place to another, according to some pretended system or alphabetical order. Thus the possessor of twenty of these collections, would find the same act repeated twenty times, and always with the same errors, and often the act required was not to be found at all.[33]

Such were the results of individual undertakings, and of the measures taken by the government to obtain a collection of the laws. From these results, it was evident, that it was necessary to recommence the whole almost from the very beginning, and consequently, first to establish certain fixed principles, and afterwards to carry them carefully into execution.

These principles were: 1st, to divide the whole collection into two epochs; the one to commence from the code of 1649, and continue

---

printed with false dates, and several ukases are merely printed in fragments; others , again, refer to a totally different period.

[33] According to the prices marked in booksellers' catalogues, the whole collection, though incomplete, cost in 1830, the sum of five thou-sand rubles.

down to December 12th, 1825, an interval of 176 years, up to the day on which the first manifest of His Imperial Majesty, now happily reigning, was published. It was thought proper to fix this period for the date of the code, because all previous laws and acts are considered by us as obsolete.[34] In assigning 'to the commencement of the second epoch the date of December 12th, 1825, it was intended to continue it by the annual publication of the laws of the preceding year.

2ly. To classify in chronological order all the legislative acts emanating from the Sovereign, or in His name, from bodies instituted by Him, without making however any distinction between laws existing and laws abrogated. Such power of selection does not belong to the order of the collection, but to that of a body of the laws.

3ly. The judicial decisions have the force of law only in those cases for which they were founded. They consequently ought not to form part of a collection of general laws. It was, however, determined to make the following exceptions to this rule: there are certain decisions whose force, according to the purport of the en-

---

[34] These laws, so important in an historical point of view, will form, under the title of Early Laws, a private collection which has been already commenced.

actment, may extend, as a case in point, to all similar cases; there are others which originally applied to some special point, but have been since taken as a precedent and guide, and have thus acquired general authority. There are private decisions which serve at the same time to interpret a general law, to affix its true signification, and to reject such interpretations as are not conformable with its spirit. It was resolved to admit in the collection all decisions of this nature. The same exception was made-regarding decisions on criminal matters. The more important of them it was considered necessary to preserve in the collection, more especially the decisions in causes relative to state crimes.

4ly. In excluding from the collection every thing of mere private or personal interest, every provisional or transitory measure, it was however deemed expedient to admit a few exceptions: there are some arrangements, essentially private and of rare occurrence, but interesting from their historical importance. It was resolved to preserve them in the collection, as memorials of by-gone ages, as a picture of the manners of social life at former periods.

These principles being established, the collection was then commenced.

The originals of the early acts being dispersed in different archives, both at Moscow and St. Petersburg, it was therefore absolutely necessary, 1st, to procure these acts, and to make tables of them; Sly, to collect the text itself, according to these tables; and Sly, I o make an accurate collection of the text so collected. [35]

---

[35] *Collection of the Tables,* 1st. In none of the archives, not even in those of the Directing Senate, were there any complete tables of the acts to be found. The number of ukases deposited in those of the preceding commission» amounted to 23,433. The archives of the Senate of St. Petersburg contained 20,742, and besides these, 445 were found in the archives of Moscow, and 8,889 in the College of War, and various other departments. Thus, the number of the acts, according to the tables, was 53,239. When these same acts were afterwards collected and compared with the register, it was discovered that the latter referred to a vast number of the acts in duplicate, under different titles and different dates, to many extracts or fragments of other ukases, and several acts which as not constituting a law, ought to have been excluded from the collection. All these errors were corrected, and the registers made to correspond faithfully with the text.

2ly. *Collection of the Text.* The original code of the Tsar Alexis, in two rolls, one containing the code itself, the other, the index of corrections made after its revision, was received from Moscow, the code as also

---

the index, are written in columns, on sheets of paper pasted one upon the other. (*A* full description of the external form of the code will be given in the history of the legislation). It is from these two manuscripts that the code was originally transcribed into a book, and afterwards printed In the Sclavonic character, in three editions, all bearing the same date of 1649. from these three, have all subsequent editions, to the number of 13, in common characters, been formed. In comparing them together, several typographical errors, and even omissions were discovered: in the present collection, the text of the three principal edition» was taken as a basis.

Copies of different acts and various tracts of former, times, all dniy certified, were afterwards received from Moscow.

The archives of the Senate of St. Petersburg, and of the Department of Inspection, sent the original register of ukases, from which the verified copies were drawn.

The cabinet of His Imperial Majesty famished 45 registers, in Which a few ukases of the time of Peter the Great and Catherine II. were found, no part of which had ever been printed.

The more recent acts which were found in the Cabinet, as well as other ukases deposited in the archives of the Holy Synod, and of different departments, were copied from the originals by functionaries appointed to examine them on the spot, and then duly verified.

Here terminated all the preliminary proceedings, and the printing was commenced.

In so vast and complicated an undertaking, success did not depend on one single commission entrusted with its execution, but on the co-operation of all the principal archives, from which the acts were to be drawn. Imperial orders were given to the heads of the different departments to effect this co-operation, and all fully

---

A vast number of documents were also examined, containing various ukases respecting the departments of the mines and salt works; of taillage and ground-rents, of external commerce, as well as touching the Department of the Interior.

Certified copies of different ukases which were not to be found in the archives of the Senate, were received from the Department of Public Roads, from the Chapter of Orders, and other institutions.

3ly. *Verification of the Text.* This verification was repeated three times: 1st, by the collation of the copies with the original acts; Sly, by the revision of functionaries particularly appointed to superintend the work; Sly, by the final revision of other functionaries, on sending the manuscripts to the press.

The formation of the collection commenced in 1826, and continued without interruption till March 1st 1830.—The printing commenced May 1st, 1828, and terminated April 1st, 1830.

responded to the call. Zeal was universally displayed, but their researches and exertions were not always attended with equal success.[36]

The first collection was followed by a second, continued on the same principles. It contains the acts from the beginning of the present reign till 1832.[37]

For convenience of research, a table of contents in chronological and alphabetical order, has been annexed to each of the two collections.

The alphabetical tables describe in full the

---

[36] Several acts, which in some archives had not been inserted in the registers, or had been omitted to be sent, did not arrive till others of the same period had been printed, and the volume completed. It was therefore found necessary to have them printed in the form of additions, at the end either of the same or of the following volume, and to connect them with the general numeral references, by means of corresponding signs. In the course of the two years which had elapsed since the publication, it has been likewise discovered, that a certain number of acts had not arrived in time. They will form a separate volume, and will be printed and published under the title of Supplement to the general Collection.

[37] The first collection is composed of 45 parts in 48 volumes; the seconds of six parts in eight volumes. Each of them is printed in 8vo, with double columns.

principal heads of all the acts: by means of these heads, not only is any particular law to be found with facility, but a general view may be obtained of the whole series of acts on any particular subject, from the very commencement down to the present time. The difficulties attending a work of this kind, comprising 48 volumes, may easily be imagined. It was necessary, in the first instance, to analyse the subject-matter of each volume, then to decompose, as it were, the constituent parts of each law, and frequently those of every article of a law, then to recompose these parts, and arrange them in a different order, by placing them under the leading head to which they referred.

The first collection, from 1643 to 1825, contains 50,920 acts; the second, from 1825 to 1832, contains 5,073. The number of acts then, in the two collections, is 55,993.

Here, the following observations naturally present themselves.

1st. The code of 1649 contains 968 articles. — Here commences our actual legislation, starting from this point, rising by degrees, dividing itself into different branches, changing its form, but always preserving its radical properties, increasing slowly but constantly, penetrating into the future in proportion as the latter expanded before it, in proportion as the national resources and public exigencies augmented, it has attained, during a course of 180 years, its full and actual development. If this development is not so extensive as in other countries, it must be remembered, in the first instance, that they have preceded us in this department by many centuries y and secondly, that on their outset they received, as has been before observed, a large inheritance consecrated by time. We, on the contrary, have been compelled to concoct almost every thing from our own private resources; so that our acquisitions are purely indigenous.

2ly. It was necessary to collect the dispersed portions of this legislation, not merely for the reason, that the body of the laws could not be otherwise formed, but also, that supposing the body of the laws to exist, their complete collection is indispensable on many occasions.

It is necessary, in the first instance, as the source of decisions in all those matters, the commencement of which refers to acts or deeds done in times antecedent to the actual laws, and which, consequently, must be judged according to the laws in force, when these acts or deeds transpired.

Secondly, the collection is necessary, in order to resolve any doubts which may arise, respecting the true sense of any article of the laws. The literal sense should be always the principal basis of the decision, but the literal sense does not always express, the spirit of a law, in all its fulness and precision: and to discover this spirit, one is often obliged to trace the law back, to the reasons upon which it was founded, arid these reasons not being designated in the articles of the body of the laws, they must be sought for at their source, in the original text from which the articles are framed. Thus, there exists, and ever must exist, an indissoluble connexion between the articles of the body of the laws, and the primitive text of a law, these two forms of one and the same legislation must be inseparable, the body of the laws being the basis' of decisions, and the text of the collection, the most simple and the most complete interpretation of the law.

Thirdly, the collection is necessary for all legislative measures where a law is to be elucidated or completed, and when it is often necessary to ascertain the precise meaning of the earlier laws, and to analyse the tenor of the whole, in order that there may be conformity, not merely with the existing spirit of the legislation, but also with the original.

Fourthly, it is known that laws are, as it were, the mirror of the internal life of a state. Through them are to be seen, the origin, the progress, the development and modification of its moral and political powers. The history of a state cannot be well understood without a knowledge of the laws, while, on the other hand, laws, without any annexed history, are often unintelligible. Thus, in proportion as a knowledge of the laws is rendered more systematic and easy, the, more accessible to contemporaries, and the more authentic to posterity, are the sources of history. It will not be superfluous here to remark, that if the publication of a complete collection of our laws, has at the present day, offered so many difficulties, the task in the course of a few years, would have been much more complicated, and might have at last become impracticable. After having, on the contrary, surmounted the first obstacles, and embraced in our circle, the whole period of 180 years, it will not henceforth be difficult, by means of annual continuations, to keep up with the current period.

II. Historical Review of the Laws.

As the collection advanced, analyses, or historical sketches, were composed on each portion of the laws. For this purpose, after having drawn out a general plan, there were formed for each of the principal parts, particular plans or summaries, in which each subject was indicated in detail, as well as its division into books, titles, chapters, and sections.

Taking these summaries as their guides, the examination of laws relating to particular subjects, was commenced. This operation was effected in two ways: the laws were first noted in the special extracts, without any difference as to their being in force or not, provided they related to the subject in question. These materials were afterwards arranged, compared together according to their chronological order, and reduced into the form of an historical treatise. It is thus, that exact notions may be found of the changes which each law had undergone, by means of abrogation, interpretation, or complement.

This preliminary work was necessary: it was to serve as a solid base for all future undertakings, but the work would have been interminable and impracticable, had it been requisite for the history of each division of the laws, to recur to the very commencement of the legislation, viz: to the code of 1649" Happily, it was unnecessary to have recourse to this means. Various portions of our legislation were form time to time renewed by regulations. These regulations are particular codifications, which contain an outline of all the preceding laws, with fewer or more alterations. Thus, in several sections, and even in whole titles, the historical sketch commenced with the regulations, that is, with acts of a more recent period, and this was the point of departure, from which they proceeded up to the present time.

There were, however, some very diffuse portions, for which it was requisite to refer to their primitive source. In the civil and penal laws, it was necessary, after dividing them into epochs, to form the most circumstantial historical summaries. In laws of this kind, there are no other means of ascertaining their subsequent changes; for frequently, it is riot with reference to the letter, but to the force and spirit of the new acts, that the earlier ones are cited, and it is, consequently, impossible to discover the variations, unless.by comparing the tenor of the one, with that of the other; and for this purpose, it is absolutely necessary to trace their historical affinities and bearings. These summaries consequently formed a separate work of great extent; it contains upwards of 11,100 articles, which will be inserted in the general history of the legislation.

IV
DEFINITIVE UNDERTAKINGS

1. Formation of the Articles of the Body of the Laws.

In proportion as the various parts of the legislation, elucidated by historical researches, attained a state of regularity and exactness, they successively passed into another period of their formation, and assumed a determinate form; namely, that of the text of the laws. This work was also divided into two compartments: in the one, the text of the *laws* being collected and purified of all foreign admixture, they were restored to their proper places in the form of articles, and thus composed separate codes. In the second, the same codes were collectively compared together. By these means, repetitions and discrepances were often discovered; they were again to be classed and systematically arranged, in order to give to the detached parts a corresponding unity. Hence it happened, that although the principal plan of the whole body remained fixed, the plans of detached portions were often changed. For one modification in the order of any single separate code, must frequently lead to that of others with which it is connected.

In composing the articles, the principles previously mentioned were observed, that is, they were compiled, for the most part, in the same terms in which they were worded in the text. The articles formed from many acts, were embodied, either in the terms of the principal act, with the necessary complement drawn from the others, or in other terms, but corresponding to the general spirit of the whole.

Under each article, are cited the sources from which it has been drawn.[38]

These references were necessary, not only for the purpose of giving to each article a legal authenticity, but also, because they offer a means of ascertaining the spirit of the law, a method of tracing it up to its origin, a guide to assist in determining the meaning in case of doubt, in short, because they afforded one of the best systems of commentaries, — a system not founded upon

---

[38] Some few articles of a transitive nature, as it were, have no reference to their origin; they are introduced simply in order to preserve a connexion between the articles.

conjecture and arbitrary deductions, but upon the simple comparison of two forms of one and the same law — its primitive and its ultimate form. The internal connexion of these two forms cannot be destroyed, without destroying the unity of the legislation itself.

In addition to these references, there are remarks inserted in some places among the articles. Some of them serve to maintain unity of plan in the body of the laws, by pointing out, in short notes, the connexion and relation of its different articles, others explain in few words, the history of a law, when it is requisite more fully to determine its true signification.

Independently of the remarks, there are in several parts supplements annexed. They contain, in the first place, practical formulas, secondly, they furnish various explanatory details, which had they been placed in the body of the text, would have obscured the meaning of the principal articles, and broken the connexion between them: by a reference to the supplement, their legal force *is* not weakened, for they are connected with the principal articles, by an express and special indication.

The number of all the articles in the body of the laws, amounts to 36,000. By adding all those in the appendices, their total amount is 42,498.[39] The number of the chapters in the whole body of the laws, is 1,499.

2. Revision and Corrections.

The order of the revision of the codes, was established in the following manner:

For the revision of the civil codes, a committee was first appointed, the Minister of Justice being president, composed of two Senators, named to this office by Imperial command, an Attorney General, a chief secretary, a director of the chancery, and a lawyer chosen by the president. There were afterwards submitted to the revision of this committee, the bodies of the laws concerning the organization of the Senate, and the department of the administration of justice, the penal laws, and lastly, the fundamental laws of the empire.

As the different parts of the body of the laws were terminated, seven committees were appointed for the revision of the different departments of the administration.

---

[39] The number of articles in the code of Jostinian, according to a probable calculation, amounts to 45,000. (See Berriat de Sl-PrIx, histoire du droit romain.

These committees, nominated among all the departments under the immediate superintendence of their directors, and under the chief control of the Ministers, were composed of the heads of the different sections, who, from a practical knowledge of the particular subject, would be most likely to be familiar with the various acts relating to their special branch.

The plan of revision to be adopted in the committee of civil laws, was determined by an Imperial rescript of April 23rd, 1828.[40] That of the other committees was also fixed by an Imperial command.[41] The order of the work was as follows:

1st. *In the Committee of Revision of the Body of Civil and Penal Laws*, the sitting generally

---

[40] It is ordered by this rescript, that a general examination of the codes be made, in order to ascertain positively, whether they are complete end exact.

[41] In the Imperial command, of July 12th 1829, given to the Minister of finance, and repealed afterwards to the other Ministers and departments, it ii said, «to examine the codes with a double view, to ascertain, whether all the laws actually hi force la each part, are expressed in their full and true import; 2ly, whether some abrogated laws have not been admitted by subsequent acts.»

commenced by reading that portion of the work which was already concluded, in presence of the compiler, and the principal of the 2nd Section.

The questions which then arose from the verbal observations of the members, were resolved by explanations, investigations, and quotations from the text of the law, or else, the articles were corrected according to the observations elicited in the same conference.

But when doubts arose which it was not possible to resolve by verbal explanations alone, then, the articles in question were separated from the rest, and submitted to a closer and more extended examination. The discussion was adjourned till the following sitting, and in the mean time, the members of the committee, the chief secretary and lawyer on one side, and the compilers on the other, made researches, extracts, and copious elucidations.

After this preparatory work, the question was either settled, or it led to new explanations, if the existing doubt was not sufficiently elucidated by these explanations; then, the observations of the committee, accompanied with an outline of the amendments, were annexed to the verbal process of the sitting, and afterwards submitted in reports to the examination of the Sovereign.

2ly. *The Order of Revision in the other Committees* was arranged, as follows: according to a previous understanding among the Ministers, the revision in the ministerial departments was divided into two heads, the one consisted of conferences between the compilers and members of the committees; according to their mutual explanations, either the doubts were resolved, or the necessary amendments were subsequently adopted. By this, detail was avoided.

In the other plan of revision, the attention of the committee was directed only: to the articles, respecting which there had been no unanimity in the conferences. Observations on these articles were drawn up, which were also presented for Imperial sanction. All the observations of the committees generally, were afterwards sent to the 2nd Section of the Emperor's Chancery. There, after comparing them with the acts and other parts of the body of the laws, as well as with the acts more recently published, new articles were compiled, or the original ones were corrected.

The number of these observations for the whole body of the laws, without counting those which were determined by verbal explanations, amounts to two thousand.

The revision which commenced in April, 1828, and continued at intervals as the codes were prepared, was completed in May, 1832.

Two circumstances are here worthy of observation.

1. During the revision, the committees appointed in the ministerial departments, imagining that some methodical measures contained in the Ministers' circulars, were requisite in the examination of the various regulations, and particularly those of the Customs, proposed to have them inserted among the articles. This demand was complied with, and in all the regulations, concerning which similar circulars were presented, their contents have been inserted in their proper places, with a reference to the circular itself, in order to confine its operation within the limits legally assigned to it.

2. In the body of the penal laws, there occurred cases in which it was necessary to make the scale of penalties determined by the earlier laws, agree with the punishments actually established for crimes of the same nature. In the course of *this* revision, these cases were examined with scrupulous attention, and when termi-

nated, it was judged necessary, besides having them collected into a comparative table, to submit them once more to the examination of the committee; and it is in accordance with all these observations that the articles were made to correspond with the table.

3. Complements and Modifications.

During the revision of the codes, and after the examination of some had been concluded, there appeared new regulations concerning different branches of the administration, by which the earlier regulations were rendered analagous and complete. They therefore found it necessary to retrace their steps, and change not only many articles in the codes, but even whole chapters and titles, in order to class the several portions under one and the same category. For this purpose, the commencement of the year 1832, was taken as a fixed period, and it was determined that all acts subsequently published, should be afterwards analysed and comprised in the continuation of the body of the laws, which was to be published in the course of 1833. As an exception to this rule, it was deemed advisable, in this present compilation, to admit of a few of the more important acts issued in the course of 1832. Such are the regulations on bills of exchange, insolvency, the organization of commercial tribunals, auctions and sales of property, and the regulations on quarantine.

4. Tables and Summaries,

Although from the division of the whole work into eight principal codes, each of which having its prescribed limits, any particular article might be found, without much difficulty of reference, it was, notwithstanding, considered desirable to have a full and complete table of contents in alphabetical order. But the execution of such a vocabulary consisting of 42,000 articles, is a task which demands much time, more particularly from the impossibility of commencing it previous to the completion of the whole work. It was consequently thought necessary, till such time as the table might be finished, partially to supply its place by means of the following auxiliaries.

Complete summaries on each part were composed, by means of which it is easy to find, if not the article itself, at least the chapter and section in which it *is* contained. In order to furnish still greater facility, all the particular summaries have been incorporated into one general summary.

To each part was annexed a chronological table, in which is noted in order of time, the date of all the acts comprised or quoted in the work, as well as the articles which correspond with them, so that, by any given act, the article itself may be easily found, and vice versa. By this means, the transition from one classified order to the other, becomes very easy, and all the advantages of memory and practice are fully maintained.

Such were the preliminary and ultimate proceedings. We have previously remarked, that the re-organization of the last commission, was commenced Jan. 51st, 1826, as being the day on which it pleased His Imperial Majesty to take under His own immediate direction, the incorporation of the laws. From that time, during a period of seven years, this undertaking has been the constant and exclusive daily occupation of functionaries expressly appointed. Reports giving a detailed account of their progress, were submitted every week for Imperial examination. It is this unvarying attention on the part of the Monarch, and the unshaken firmness of His Sovereign will, that could alone ensure and guarantee the success of the undertaking, the execution of which, surrounded by difficulties, had remained for a century, vacillating and uncertain. Every part of the body of the laws, as soon as it was completed, was presented to the examination of His Majesty; and it was afterwards subjected to the revision assigned it, according to the system above mentioned. The first code (the Organic Laws) was submitted to the press in the beginning of 1832, and about the end of the same year, all the eight codes, forming fifteen volumes, were printed. On the 31st Jany, 1833, a Manifest of His Imperial Majesty announced the completion of the work, and determined the rules to be observed in its practical application, and the grounds of its legal authority.

Before we conclude this summary, it may not be thought superfluous, here to add a brief article concerning the bodies of the Provincial Laws.

It is known that it had been for some time in contemplation, to extricate the Special Laws of the Governments of the Baltic, from their existing state of confusion. To effect this, different measures were adopted at the time, but they were never followed by any decided result. This idea was revived in 1804, when the commission for forming the code was appointed. We have elsewhere remarked (in the first part of this summary) that local committees were formed both for the Governments of the Baltic, and for the Western Provinces. The causes of the small success which accompanied their establishment, have also been explained.

In 1850, H. M. the Emperor thought proper to direct the 2nd Section of His Chancery, to make two separate compilations; one, for the incorporation of the laws of the Governments of the Baltic, the other, for that of the Western Provinces. The work was consigned to well informed and experienced functionaries, who were furnished with plans and every requisite assistance. By the union of these measures, the body of the laws belonging to the Governments of the Baltic, has been rendered capable of being advanced to the first step of local revision. The body of laws for the Western Provinces will be terminated in the course of the present year, and when completed, will undergo a revision. These two works, therefore, are now in progress, and we have reason to hope that they will be happily accomplished.

MANIFEST

OF HIS IMPERIAL MAJESTY. BY THE GRACE OF GOD, WE, NICHOLAS THE FIRST, emperor and autocrat of all the russian, etc., etc., etc.

Having acknowledged, on Our accession to the throne, the indispensable necessity of arranging the Body of the Laws of Our country in a clear and systematic order, We have commanded, in the first place, that a full and complete collection of them be formed and published, and We have declared Our will that all the laws actually in force though out Our Empire, be afterwards extracted from this collection, to be incorporated into a uniform and regular Code of Law, without, in any respect changing their spirit; the work to be guided by and based upon the groundwork adopted by Peter the Great, in 1709.

The first part of this plan was terminated in 1830.

At present, by the assistance of the Almighty, after seven years of unremitting exertion carried on under Our own immediate direction, the second part has been recently accomplished. From the publication of the Code of 1649, *down* to January 1st, 1832, all the laws enacted during this interval of one hundred and eighty three years, and which, notwithstanding the changes introduced by time, have preserved their force and tenor up to the present period, have been embodied according the nature of the subject-matter to which they referred, all the enactments abrogated by subsequent *laws* have been rescinded, with the exception of the regulations respecting the land and sea forces, and a few others enumerated below, all these laws have been digested into one uniform system, united into one single body, divided into Codes, according to the principal divisions of administrative and judicial proceedings. Every methodical enactment issued subsequent to January 1st, 1832, or those which in the ordinary course of legislation shall hereafter be published, shall annually form an annexed supplement to the Body of the Laws, according to the order of these same Codes, and with references to their articles, so that the general system of the Laws once established, may continue to preserve its unity and agreement.

Justice and regularity in the administration, the most pressing and most essential requirements of the Empire, imperatively demanded this measure.

It guarantees the force and operation of the Laws for the present, and establishes a solid foundation for gradual perfection, as regards the future. In a word, it realizes that which Our ancestors ardently desired, for an almost uninterrupted period of one hundred and twenty-six years.

In addressing by this Present, these Codes of Laws to the Directing Senate, We order the following arrangements, as to what regards their force and legal authority.

1. The Body of Laws shall come into operation January 1st, 1835.

2. The legal force of the Body of the Laws shall consist from that time, in its articles being literally pleaded and quoted in all administrative and judicial cases, consequently, on every occasion where the Laws are to be quoted in the preliminaries of a cause and the motives of a decision, whether textually, or by extracts, or by their title only, the articles of the Body of the Laws corresponding with the particular subject-matter, must be referred to, adduced and quoted

in all cases which occur on, or after, the first of January, 1835.

3. All the ukases and regulations issued since January 1st, 1832, not being comprehended in the existing Body of the Laws, as well as those which may be afterwards enacted, shall be cited and pleaded immediately by their date and title, until they have been inserted in the annual supplements. Shall be also directly quoted:

1st. All Provincial Laws, in all places where they are in force, until they have been collected into Special Codes by means of measures adopted for that purpose.

2ly. Laws concerning Public Instruction and the Control of the Empire, the intended reorganization of these branches, not having as yet admitted the completion of these regulations by which they are to be controlled.

3ly. Laws and regulations concerning Foreign Confessions.

4. Seeing that the collection of the Laws in one complete body of legislation, produces no alteration either in their application, or general tenour, but introduces order and uniformity into the collective body, where cases of doubt therefore arise respecting the meaning of the law, whether from its insufficiency or total silence, then, in order to obtain the interpretation, or the

necessary addition, the system in actual operation according to the regulations shall be adopted as a guide.

The Directing Senate shall make every arrangement necessary for insuring the execution of this Present:

Given at St. Petersburg, the thirty-first day of the month of January, in the year of Our Lord, one thousand eight hundred and thirty three, and the eighth of Our reign.

Signed: ***NICHOLAS***.

Countersigned: Prince V. Kotchoubey,
President of the Council of the Empire.

TABLE

Of the number of Statutes, Organizations, Instructions, Diplomas, Ukases, and Treatises, published between the Code of January 1649, and January 1st, 1832.

FIRST COLLECTION. *(From Jan. 29th 1649, till Dec. 12th 1825).*		Length of Reign.	Number of Statutes, Regulations. and Instructs.	Number Of Diplomas.	Number of Manifests and Ukases.	Number of Treatises.	Total.
		Years mths.					
I.	Reign of the Tsar Alexis.	27	16	45	509	48	618
II.	Tsar Theodore.	6 – 3	17	16	258	4	295
III.	Tsars John and Peter.	13 – 9	17	25	563	18	623
IV.	Emperor Peter I.	29	134	27	2861	88	3110
V.	Empress Catherine I.	2 – 4	5	2	415	6	428
VI.	Emperor Peter II	2 – 8	2	2	414	10	428
VII.	Empress Anne.	10 – 9	45	19	2683	20	2767
VIII.	Regency of the Ex-Duke of Courland and of the Princess Anne of Brunswick-Luneburg.	1 – 1	2	9	194	6	211
IX.	Reign of the Empress Elisabeth.	20 – 1	26	20	2842	34	2922

X. Emperor Peter III.	33 – 5	1	–	189	2	192
XI. Empress CatherineII.	6	118	33	5771	35	5957
XII. Emperor Paul I.	4 - 2½	50	15	2170	15	2250
XIII. Emperor AlexanderI.	24-8½	386	28	10619	86	11119
SECOND COLLECTION. *(From Dec. 12th 1825, till Jan. 1st 1832).*	175-9	819	241	29488	372	30920
XIV. Reign of His Imperial Majesty NICHOLAS I.	6 - 1	207	9	4845	12	5073
Total	181-10	1026	250	34335	384	35993

Made in the USA
Monee, IL
04 November 2026

67384997R00059